Explore the
coral Reef

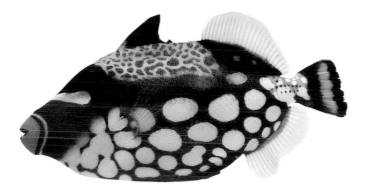

Explora el
arrecife de coral

FIRST EDITION

Series Editor Deborah Lock; **US Senior Editor** Shannon Beatty; **Editor** Arpita Nath;
Design Assistant Sadie Thomas; **Art Editor** Dheeraj Arora; **Senior Art Editor** Tory Gordon-Harris;
Producer Sara Hu; **Pre-Production Producer** Nadine King; **Jacket Designer** Natalie Godwin;
Managing Editor Soma Chowdhury; **Managing Art Editor** Ahlawat Gunjan;
Art Directors Rachel Foster and Martin Wilson; **Reading Consultant** Linda Gambrell, PhD

THIS EDITION

Editorial Management by Oriel Square
Produced for DK by WonderLab Group LLC
Jennifer Emmett, Erica Green, Kate Hale, *Founders*

Editors Grace Hill Smith, Libby Romero, Michaela Weglinski; **Spanish Translation** Isabel C. Mendoza;
Photography Editors Kelley Miller, Annette Kiesow, Nicole DiMella;
Managing Editor Rachel Houghton; **Designers** Project Design Company; **Researcher** Michelle Harris;
Copy Editor Lori Merritt; **Indexer** Connie Binder; **Proofreaders** Carmen Orozco, Larry Shea;
Reading Specialist Dr. Jennifer Albro; **Curriculum Specialist** Elaine Larson

Published in the United States by DK Publishing
1745 Broadway, 20th Floor, New York, NY 10019
Copyright © 2023 Dorling Kindersley Limited
DK, a Division of Penguin Random House LLC
23 24 25 26 27 10 9 8 7 6 5 4 3 2 1
001-336111-Aug/2023

A catalog record for this book
is available from the Library of Congress.
HC ISBN: 978-0-7440-8381-1
PB ISBN: 978-0-7440-8380-4

DK books are available at special discounts when purchased
in bulk for sales promotions, premiums, fundraising, or
educational use. For details, contact: DK Publishing Special Markets,
1745 Broadway, 20th Floor, New York, NY 10019
SpecialSales@dk.com

Printed and bound in China

The publisher would like to thank the following for their kind permission to reproduce their images:
a=above; c=center; b=below; l=left; r=right; t=top; b/g=background

Dorling Kindersley: Tina Gong 10c; **Dreamstime.com:** Luca Gialdini 20, Ingrid Prats / Titania1980 3;
Getty Images / iStock: strmko 4-5; **Shutterstock.com:** Sergius Bleicher 24-25, Rich Carey 10-11, Diman_Diver 21,
Rostislav Stefanek 26-27, Stock for you 19cra
Cover images: *Front:* **Dreamstime.com:** John Anderson b, Artisticco Llc; *Back:* **Dreamstime.com:** Andrii Symonenko bl
All other images © Dorling Kindersley

For the curious
Para los curiosos
www.dk.com

Explore the coral Reef

Explora el arrecife de coral

Deborah Lock

Contents
Contenido

6   Coral
El coral

8   Sea Turtles
Las tortugas marinas

10   Seahorses
Los caballitos de mar

13   Sea Stars
Las estrellas de mar

14   Jellyfish
Las medusas

16   Sharks
Los tiburones

18   Octopuses
Los pulpos

20 Crabs
Los cangrejos

22 Rays
Las rayas

24 Dolphins
Los delfines

26 Eels
Las anguilas

30 Glossary
Glosario

31 Index
Índice

32 Quiz
Prueba

Coral
El coral

Here is a coral reef.

Esto es un arrecife de coral.

What animals do you see?
¿Qué animales ves?

coral
coral

fish
pez

Sea Turtles
Las tortugas marinas

The sea turtles play in the ocean.

Las tortugas marinas juegan en el océano.

shell
caparazón

flipper
aleta

Seahorses
Los caballitos de mar

The seahorses sway
to and fro.

Los caballitos de mar se
balancean hacia adelante
y hacia atrás.

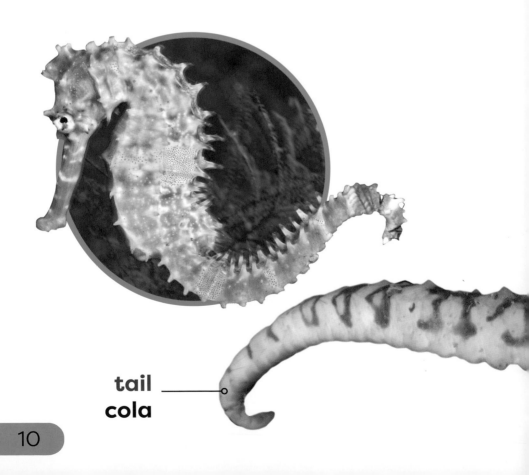

tail ——o
cola

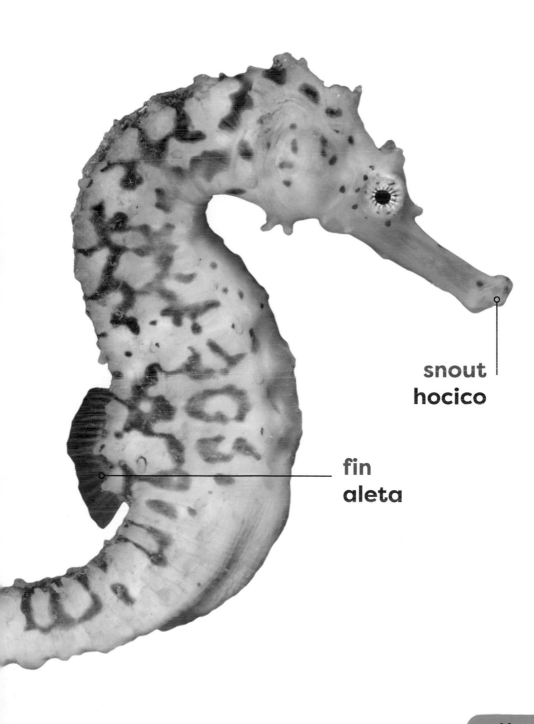

snout
hocico

fin
aleta

arm
brazo

Sea Stars
Las estrellas de mar

Sea stars crawl
on the ocean floor.

Las estrellas de mar se
arrastran en el suelo marino.

Jellyfish
Las medusas

Jellyfish float up and down in the ocean.

Las medusas flotan en el océano hacia arriba y hacia abajo.

tentacles
tentáculos

bell
campana

tail
cola

Sharks
Los tiburones

Here comes a shark.
It looks for food.

Aquí viene un tiburón.
Está buscando comida.

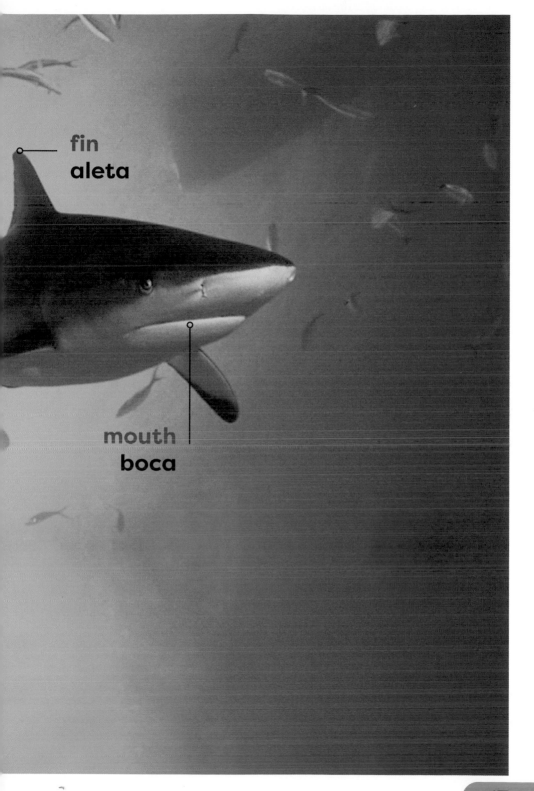

fin
aleta

mouth
boca

Octopuses
Los pulpos

An octopus shoots off to hide.

Un pulpo se impulsa con fuerza para esconderse.

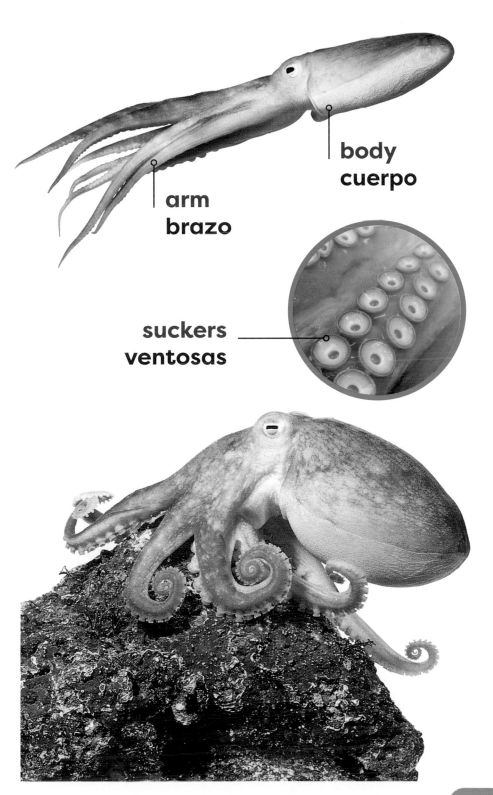

arm
brazo

body
cuerpo

suckers
ventosas

Crabs
Los cangrejos

Crabs hide in the coral and inside big shells.

Los cangrejos se esconden en el coral y dentro de grandes conchas.

shell
caparazón

leg
pata

claw
tenaza

Rays
Las rayas

A ray hides on the ocean floor.

Una raya se esconde en el suelo marino.

hiding
esconderse

eye
ojo

fin
aleta

tail
cola

Dolphins
Los delfines

A dolphin swims away. It moves its tail up and down.

Un delfín pasa nadando. Mueve su cola hacia arriba y hacia abajo.

mouth
boca

tail
cola

flipper
aleta

Eels
Las anguilas

An eel looks out
for the shark.

Una anguila está atenta
por si aparece un tiburón.

eye
ojo

fin
aleta

tail
cola

The shark swims away.

El tiburón pasa nadando.

gills
branquias

nose
nariz

Glossary
Glosario

eel
a snake-like fish

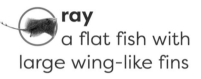 **octopus**
a sea animal with
eight long arms

ray
a flat fish with
large wing-like fins

sea star
a sea animal with
five arms shaped like
a star

 sea turtle
a marine reptile
with a domed shell

anguila
pez que parece
una serpiente

estrella de mar
animal marino
con cinco brazos que
forman una estrella

pulpo
animal marino
con ocho brazos largos

 **raya**
pez aplanado
con aletas largas que
parecen alas

tortuga marina
reptil marino
con un caparazón
redondeado

Index
Índice

claw   21
coral   6, 7, 20
crabs   20
dolphins   24
eels   26
fin   11, 17, 23, 27
fish   7
flipper   9, 25
gills   29
jellyfish   14
octopuses   18

rays   22
sea stars   13
sea turtles   8
seahorses   10
sharks   16, 26, 28
shell   8, 20, 21
snout   11
tail   10, 16, 23, 24, 25, 27
tentacles   14
turtles   8

aleta   9, 11, 17, 23, 25, 27
anguilas   26
branquias   29
caballitos de mar   10
cangrejos   20
caparazón   8, 21
cola   10, 16, 23, 24, 25, 27
conchas   20
coral   6, 7, 20
delfines   24
estrellas de mar   13

hocico   11
medusas   14
pez   7
pulpos   18
rayas   22
tenaza   21
tentáculos   14
tiburones   16, 26, 28
tortugas   8
tortugas marinas   8

Quiz
Prueba

Answer the questions to see what you have learned.
Check your answers with an adult.

Which sea animal am I?

1. I have flippers and a hard shell.
2. I have a bell and tentacles.
3. I have long arms covered in suckers.
4. I hide in coral and inside big shells.
5. I am a fish with a long
   tail and small fins.

1. A sea turtle 2. A jellyfish 3. An octopus 4. A crab 5. An eel

Responde las preguntas para saber cuánto aprendiste.
Verifica tus respuestas con un adulto.

¿Qué animal marino soy?

1. Tengo aletas y un caparazón duro.
2. Tengo una campana y tentáculos.
3. Tengo brazos largos cubiertos de ventosas.
4. Me escondo en el coral y dentro de
   grandes conchas.
5. Soy un pez de cola larga y pequeñas aletas.

1. Una tortuga marina 2. Una medusa 3. Un pulpo 4. Un cangrejo
5. Una anguila